THE WORLD'S GREATEST
WARPLANES

Ian Graham

Raintree

4 741241 000

www.raintreepublishers.co.uk
Visit our website to find out more information about Raintree books.

To order:
☎ Phone 44 (0) 1865 888112
▤ Send a fax to 44 (0) 1865 314091
▯ Visit the Raintree Bookshop at www.raintreepublishers.co.uk to browse our
catalogue and order online.

First published in Great Britain by Raintree,
Halley Court, Jordan Hill, Oxford, OX2 8EJ, part
of Harcourt Education.
Raintree is a registered trademark of Harcourt
Education Ltd.

Editorial: Andrew Farrow and Dan Nunn
Design: Ron Kamen and Philippa Baile
Picture Research: Hannah Taylor and Elaine
 Willis
Production: Victoria Fitzgerald

Originated by Dot Gradations Ltd.
Printed in China

The paper used to print this book comes from
sustainable resources.

ISBN 13: 978 1844 212675 (HB)
ISBN 10: 1 844 21267 X (HB)
10 09 08 07 06
10 9 8 7 6 5 4 3 2 1

ISBN 13: 978 1844 212866 (PB)
ISBN 10: 1 844 21286 6 (PB)
10 09 08 07
10 9 8 7 6 5 4 3 2 1

**British Library Cataloguing in Publication
Data**
Graham, Ian
  Warplanes. – (The world's greatest)
  1. Airplanes, Military – Juvenile literature
  I. Title
  623.7'46
A full catalogue record for this book is
available from the British Library.

Acknowledgements
The publishers would like to thank the
following for permission to reproduce
photographs:

Associated Press pp. **7**, **10**, **11 bottom**,
13 right, **16**, **25 top**; Corbis pp. **4 top**
(Bettmann), **4 bottom** (Bettmann), **5**
(Rob Sachs), **6** (Reuters), **9**, **11 top**
(Reuters/Denis Balibouse), **13 left** (Reuters),
12 (John H. Clark), **14** (Roger Ressmeyer),
15 bottom (Sygma/Ron Sachs), **18** (Aaron
Allmon II/U.S. Air Force), **19** (Aero Graphics,
Inc.), **20** (George Hall), **21** (Reuters), **22**
(Aero Graphics, Inc.), **23 top** (Reuters),
23 bottom (George Hall), **24** (George Hall),
25 bottom (Reuters); DOD Photo by Senior
Airman Diane S. Robinson/U.S. Air Force
pp. **1**, **17**; Flight Collection pp. **8**, **15 top**.

Cover photograph of an F-22 Raptor
reproduced with permission of Getty Images/
Judson Broehme, U.S. Air Force.

Every effort has been made to contact
copyright holders of any material reproduced
in this book. Any omissions will be rectified in
subsequent printings if notice is given to the
publishers.

Contents

Words appearing in the text in bold, **like this**, are explained in the Glossary.

Warplanes

The first warplanes were built nearly 100 years ago. They were small planes made from wood and covered with fabric. They were powered by engines like car engines, and had **propellers**. Most of them had two wings, one above the other. Some were small fighters armed with guns, which attacked other planes. Others were bigger planes, called bombers. These dropped bombs on enemies below.

The British Sopwith Camel was the greatest fighter of World War I (1914–1918). Sopwith Camels shot down more enemy aircraft than any other fighters in the war.

*The American P-51 Mustang was armed with six **machine guns** inside its wings. Its powerful engine and **sleek** shape made it one of the best fighters of World War II (1939–1945).*

Modern warplanes

Since then, warplanes have become faster and more deadly. Modern warplanes are made from metal or new materials like **carbon fibre**. They have **jet engines** that make them amazingly fast. The fastest warplanes can fly faster than the speed of sound. Warplanes today also carry more weapons than ever.

15 m/49 ft 2 in

The American F-16 Fighting Falcon is one of the world's best modern combat planes. It can fly more than ten times faster than a Sopwith Camel!

	Sopwith Camel	**F-16 Fighting Falcon**
Date:	1917	1979
Made from:	Wood and canvas	Metal
Length:	5.7 m/18 ft 9 in	15 m/49 ft 2 in
Wingspan:	8.5 m/28 ft	10 m/32 ft 9 in
Top speed:	180 kph/110 mph	2,415 kph/1,500 mph
Weapons:	2 machine guns	1 cannon and up to 9,275 kg/ 20,405 lb of other bombs and missiles

The world's best warplane

One of the newest warplanes is the American F-22 Raptor. It is designed to be the best fighter in the world. It can detect enemy planes and shoot them down before their pilots even know the F-22 is there.

Super speeder

When warplanes fly faster than sound, their engines use up fuel very quickly. For this reason, warplanes usually fly at very high speeds only in short bursts. The F-22's engines are specially designed so that it can fly faster than sound for a long time.

Computer control

The F-22 is a very complicated machine. The pilot needs the help of computers to keep it under control. It is designed this way so that when the pilot turns the plane, it can turn amazingly fast. This makes it hard for enemy fighters to attack it.

*The F-22 keeps its smooth shape by storing bombs and **missiles** inside its body. Extra weapons like this missile can be carried under its wings if necessary.*

Which is best?

The F-22 is designed to battle with the world's leading fighters, including Russia's Sukhoi Su-27. The Su-27 is a bit bigger and has more weapons, but the F-22 is faster, more advanced, and harder to detect.

Warplanes like the F-22 are painted dull grey to make them hard to see against grey clouds.

	F-22	Su-27
Crew:	1	1
Engines:	2	2
Length:	18.9 m/62 ft 1 in	21.9 m/71 ft 11 in
Height:	5 m/16 ft 5 in	5.9 m/19 ft 5 in
Wingspan:	13.6 m/44 ft 7 in	14.7 m/48 ft 2 in
Top speed:	2,180 kph/1,355 mph	2,500 kph/1,555 mph
Weapons:	20-mm cannon and 8 missiles	30-mm cannon and 10 missiles

The fastest warplanes

The MiG-25 is a Russian warplane designed to stop the fastest bombers. It flies at 3,000 kph/1,865 mph so that it can meet enemy bombers before they reach their targets. It can fly so fast because it has two very powerful jet engines and a smooth shape like a dart. The MiG-25 is also known as the Foxbat.

At top speed, the MiG-25 flies nearly a kilometre (over half a mile) every second!

FASTER THAN A JUMBO JET!
The fastest warplanes are more than three times faster than a jet airliner.

car 200 kph / 125 mph

jumbo jet 900 kph / 560 mph

MiG-25 Foxbat 3,000 kph / 1,865 mph

SR-71 Blackbird 3,529 kph / 2,193 mph

The Blackbird

The fastest jet-plane ever built was the US Lockheed SR-71 Blackbird spy-plane. It was designed to fly so fast and high that no other plane could attack it. On 28 July 1976, it set a speed record of 3,529 kph/2,193 mph. It is still the fastest speed reached by any jet-plane.

The SR-71 Blackbird could fly so high that its crew had to wear spacesuits!

	MiG-25 Foxbat	Lockheed SR-71 Blackbird
Crew:	1	2
Engines:	2	2
Length:	22.3 m/73 ft 2 in	32.7 m/107 ft 5 in
Wingspan:	14.1 m/46 ft 3 in	16.9 m/55 ft 7 in
Top speed:	3,000 kph/1,865 mph	3,529 kph/2,193 mph
Greatest height:	20,700 m/67,915 ft	25,900 m/85,000 ft
Weapons:	Up to six missiles	None

The biggest warplanes

The Antonov An-124 Condor is a giant military cargo plane. It is used by the Russian air force to carry the biggest and heaviest cargoes. The Condor is about the same size as the biggest Jumbo Jet aeroplane. It can carry up to 150 tonnes of cargo. Fully loaded, the plane and its cargo can weigh up to 405 tonnes – that's as much as 300 family cars!

	Antonov An-124 Condor	Boeing 747-400
Crew:	up to 7	2 plus cabin crew 4
Engines:	4	4
Length:	69.1 m/226 ft 8 in	70.7 m/231 ft 10 in
Wingspan:	73.3 m/240 ft 6 in	64.4 m/211 ft 5 in
Maximum cargo:	150,000 kg/330,695 lb	up to 524 people
Weapons:	None	None

The Condor can also be used to transport people. In an emergency, up to 500 people can squeeze into its cargo bay.

The double-decker plane

The Condor is unusual because it has two decks. The top deck contains the **cockpit** and a cabin with 88 seats. The lower deck is an enormous cargo bay big enough to carry tanks and helicopters. The Condor's nose can swing up and its tail opens. This means that loading can start at one end before unloading has finished at the other end.

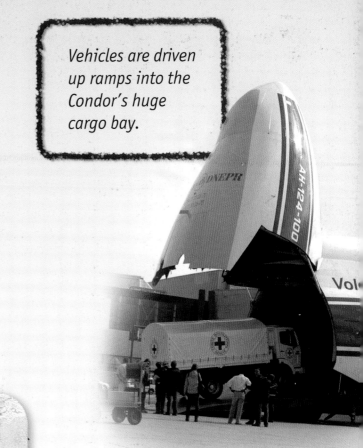

Vehicles are driven up ramps into the Condor's huge cargo bay.

KNEELING PLANE

The Condor can "kneel down" closer to the ground to make it easier for vehicles to drive inside.

An even bigger plane was developed from the An-124, called the Antonov An-225. Only one was ever built. It was used to transport Russia's space shuttle.

Clever fliers

Some warplanes can take off straight up into the air. This means they can take off and land from fields, roads, and ships.

Swivelling jets

The Harrier is a **fighter-bomber**. It can **hover** in the air like a bumblebee! The jet from the engine comes out of four pipes, or nozzles. There are two at the front and two at the back. When they point down, they push the plane upwards. Then the pilot swivels them back and they push the plane forwards.

The Harrier was nicknamed the "Jump-jet", because it can jump straight into the air.

FUEL SAVER
Taking off straight upwards burns a lot of fuel, so the Harrier often uses a short take-off run.

Tilting engines

The American V-22 Osprey aircraft does a different job from the Harrier. It carries soldiers and cargo. Its engines point upwards for take-off. The spinning **rotor** blades lift it straight up into the air. Then the engines tilt down and the plane flies forwards.

The secret of the Osprey's flying ability is its tilting engines. The photo on the top left shows the engines pointing upwards for take-off and landing. The photo on the bottom right shows the engines in position for flying forwards.

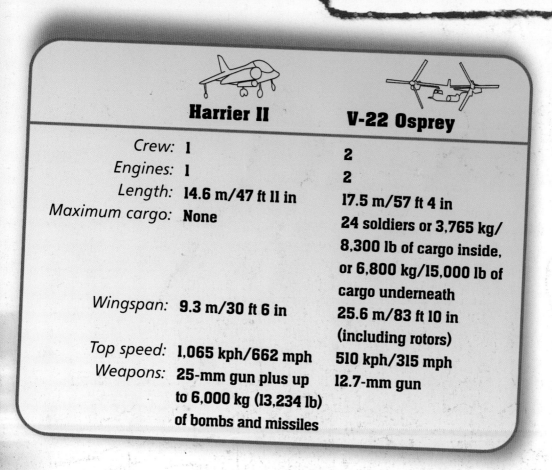

	Harrier II	V-22 Osprey
Crew:	1	2
Engines:	1	2
Length:	14.6 m/47 ft 11 in	17.5 m/57 ft 4 in
Maximum cargo:	None	24 soldiers or 3,765 kg/ 8,300 lb of cargo inside, or 6,800 kg/15,000 lb of cargo underneath
Wingspan:	9.3 m/30 ft 6 in	25.6 m/83 ft 10 in (including rotors)
Top speed:	1,065 kph/662 mph	510 kph/315 mph
Weapons:	25-mm gun plus up to 6,000 kg (13,234 lb) of bombs and missiles	12.7-mm gun

The strangest warplane

The US B-2 Spirit bomber is one of the strangest planes you'll ever see. It has no tail or body – it's just one big wing! The crew sits inside a cockpit on top. Four jet engines are hidden inside bulges on either side of the cockpit. The B-2 is designed to fly safely over the most dangerous places.

The B-2 bomber's engines are on top of its wings. This hides them from enemy radar on the ground.

Northrop B-2 Spirit

Crew:	2 or 3
Engines:	4
Length:	21 m/69 ft
Height:	5.2 m/17 ft
Wingspan:	52.4 m/172 ft
Top speed:	765 kph/475 mph
Weapons:	18,145 kg/40,000 lb of bombs and missiles

The invisible plane

Did you know that armies use **radar** to see enemy planes before they arrive? The B-2 is made so that its strange shape will confuse enemy radar. If enemies cannot see the B-2 coming, they cannot attack it. Planes like the B-2 that are hard to find are called stealth planes.

21 m/69 ft

LIKE A BIRD

On radar, the B-2 looks as small as a bird.

The B-2 Spirit bomber is called a flying wing.

Other unusual warplanes

Some warplanes can look odd because of what they are designed to do. The US Lockheed F-117 Nighthawk and Boeing E-3 Sentry planes certainly look unusual!

Invisible attacker

The F-117 Nighthawk is a stealth plane, like the B-2 bomber. It is designed to be hard for its enemies to find by radar. The Nighthawk is designed to attack heavily defended targets on the ground. It is smaller than the B-2.

The Nighthawk can fly itself for most of its mission! The pilot takes over only when the target is in sight.

	F-117 Nighthawk	Boeing E-3 Sentry
Crew:	1	up to 21
Engines:	2	4
Length:	19.4 m/63 ft 9 in	46.6 m/152 ft 11 in
Height:	3.9 m/12 ft 9 in	12.5 m/41 ft 9 in
Wingspan:	13.2 m/43 ft 4 in	44.4 m/145 ft 9 in
Top speed:	1,040 kph/645 mph	850 kph/530 mph
Weapons:	2,268 kg/5,000 lb of bombs or missiles	None

The flying sentry

The Boeing E-3 Sentry's job is to fly above a battle and watch everything that happens below it. A spinning radar disc on top of the plane can detect aircraft up to 320 kilometres (200 miles) away. The Sentry is crammed with equipment that works out which planes are friendly and which are enemies. It then guides friendly fighter-planes toward the enemy aircraft.

LONG-TIME FLIER

The E-3 Sentry can keep flying for 11 hours, or even longer if it's re-fuelled in the air.

A Boeing E-3 touches down after another secret mission.

The most deadly warplane

The American F-15 is possibly the world's most deadly warplane, because it can do more than one job very well. It was designed to be the world's best fighter. It can slice through the air at more than twice the speed of sound to meet enemy planes. But it is not just very fast. When it has to fight other planes, it can turn and climb very quickly. This makes it a very hard plane to catch.

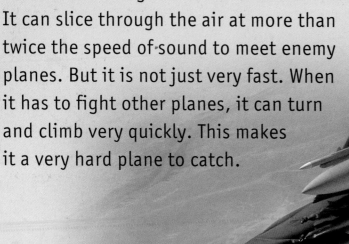

An F-15 fighter drops hot, bright flares to confuse enemy missiles.

FAST CLIMBER

The F-15E climbs so quickly that it could reach the top of Mount Everest, the world's tallest mountain, in less than one minute! Mount Everest is over 8,800 metres (29,000 feet) tall.

19.4 m/63 ft 9 in

*The F-15E has two cockpits –
the front for the pilot and the
back for the weapons officer.
Its bombs and missiles hang
underneath it.*

Fighter-bomber

The first F-15s were used only as fighters to attack other
planes. The latest F-15, called the F-15E Strike Eagle, is
also a bomber. Look at the table below that compares it
to a 1940s bomber like the B-17. The Strike Eagle is more
than five times faster, can carry four times the weight of
bombs, and needs a smaller crew than the B-17.

	F-15E Strike Eagle	**B-17G Flying Fortress**
Crew:	2	10
Engines:	2	4
Length:	19.4 m/63 ft 9 in	22.8 m/74 ft 9 in
Wingspan:	13.1 m/42 ft 10 in	31.6 m/103 ft 10 in
Top speed:	2,655 kph/1,650 mph	485 kph/300 mph
Weapons:	20-mm gun and up to 11,000 kg/24,250 lb of bombs and missiles	13 machine guns and up to 2,725 kg/6,000 lb of bombs

Other deadly warplanes

There are many other deadly warplanes in use around the world. These include the fearsome AH-64 Apache military helicopter, and advanced fighters like the Eurofighter Typhoon.

Apache attack

The American AH-64 Apache is an attack helicopter. Its job is to attack targets on the ground with rockets and missiles. It also has a powerful gun under its nose. The Apache can hover behind trees, then pop up to fire at enemy vehicles. The Apache works close to the ground, so it is likely to be shot at. It is fitted with thick sheets of armour to protect the crew inside.

Rockets and missiles are carried in pods on each side of the Apache.

gun

rocket

missiles

JOINING FORCES

Four European countries worked together to build the Eurofighter – Britain, Germany, Italy, and Spain.

Eurofighter Typhoon

The Eurofighter Typhoon is called a multi-role fighter because it can be used in several ways. It can be a fighter. It can also help soldiers by attacking enemy forces on the ground. And it can attack ships at sea. Each of these missions needs different weapons, so the Typhoon can be armed with a variety of different bombs and missiles.

canard

*The Eurofighter has small wings, called **canards**, on its nose. These help it to turn quickly during air battles.*

	AH-64 Apache	Eurofighter Typhoon
Crew:	2	1
Engines:	2	2
Length:	17.8 m/58 ft 3 in	16.0 m/52 ft 4 in
Wingspan:	14.6 m/48 ft (rotor diameter)	11.0 m/35 ft 11 in
Top speed:	260 kph/160 mph	2,125 kph/1,320 mph
Weapons:	30-mm cannon plus rockets and missiles	27-mm gun and up to 6,500 kg/14,330 lb of bombs and missiles

The most destructive warplane

The US B-52 Stratofortress bomber was designed in the 1950s to fly thousands of kilometres and drop nuclear bombs from a great height. Fortunately, there have been no nuclear wars! Now it is used to drop ordinary bombs and missiles. The B-52 has a big space inside it for carrying lots of bombs. This is called the **bomb bay**. More bombs and missiles can be carried underneath the B-52's long wings.

B-52H Stratofortress

Crew:	6
Engines:	8
Length:	48.6 m/159 ft 5 in
Height:	12.4 m/40 ft 8 in
Wingspan:	56.3 m/185 ft
Top speed:	1,050 kph/650 mph
Weapons:	20-mm cannon and 31,750 kg/70,000 lb of bombs and missiles

The B-52's engines are housed in pods under the wings. There are two engines to each pod.

engines in pods

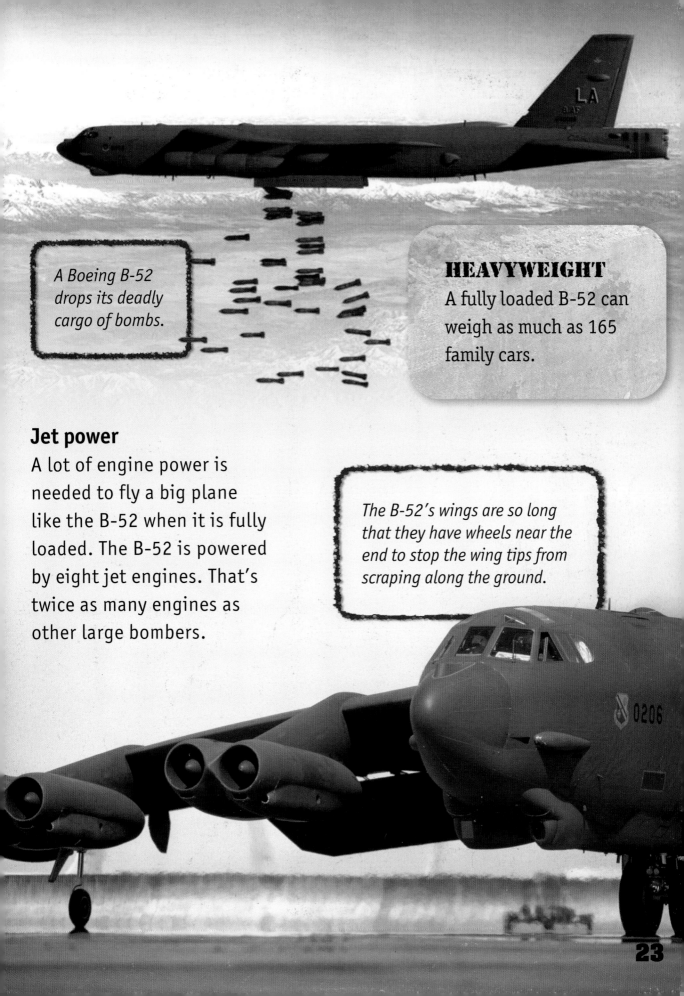

A Boeing B-52 drops its deadly cargo of bombs.

HEAVYWEIGHT

A fully loaded B-52 can weigh as much as 165 family cars.

Jet power

A lot of engine power is needed to fly a big plane like the B-52 when it is fully loaded. The B-52 is powered by eight jet engines. That's twice as many engines as other large bombers.

The B-52's wings are so long that they have wheels near the end to stop the wing tips from scraping along the ground.

Other hard hitters

Warplanes like the B-52 Stratofortress (see pages 22–23) are designed to deliver a shattering blow to the enemy. But hard-hitters come in many shapes and sizes. This is because they are designed to do different jobs.

Armour attack

The American A-10 Thunderbolt attacks tanks and other armoured vehicles. It is armed with the most powerful gun ever fitted to an aircraft, a 30-mm cannon with seven barrels!

The A-10 looks mean and ugly, so it is also sometimes called the "warthog".

	A-10 Thunderbolt	**Tu-160 Blackjack**	**AC-130U Spectre Gunship**
Crew:	1	4	13
Engines:	2	4	4
Length:	16.3 m/53 ft 6 in	54.1 m/177 ft 6 in	29.8 m/97 ft 9 in
Wingspan:	17.5 m/57 ft 5 in	55.7 m/182 ft 9 in	40.4 m/132 ft 7 in
Top speed:	700 kph/435 mph	2,000 kph/1,245 mph	480 kph/300 mph
Weapons:	30-mm cannon and 7,260kg/16,000 lb of bombs and missiles	16,500 kg/36,376 lb of bombs and missiles	25-mm, 40-mm, and 105-mm cannon

*The **supersonic** Tu-160 Blackjack bomber can fly faster than many fighters.*

The Blackjack

The Russian Tupolev Tu-160 Blackjack bomber is the world's largest bomber and heaviest combat aircraft. The Blackjack is a swing-wing plane. As it flies, its wings swing back further to help it fly faster.

The AC-130U Spectre is called a gunship because its main weapons are guns. The warplane in this photo is an earlier version of the Spectre – the AC-130H.

Facts and figures

There are hundreds of warplanes. Some of the fastest, biggest, and most deadly are listed here. If you want to know more about these or other warplanes, look on pages 30 and 31 to find out how to do some research.

FIGHTERS

Name and country	Length	Wingspan	Top speed
Eurofighter Typhoon (Europe)	16.0 m/52 ft 4 in	11.0 m/35 ft 11 in	2,125 kph/1,320 mph
F-14 Tomcat (USA)	19.1 m/62 ft 8 in	19.5 m/64 ft 2 in	1,995 kph/1,240 mph
F-15E Strike Eagle (USA)	19.4 m/63 ft 9 in	13.1 m/42 ft 10 in	2,655 kph/1,650 mph
F-16 Fighting Falcon (USA)	15.0 m/49 ft 2 in	10.0 m/32 ft 9 in	2,415 kph/1,500 mph
F/A-18 Super Hornet (USA)	18.3 m/60 ft 1 in	13.6 m/44 ft 7 in	1,910 kph/1,190 mph
F-22 Raptor (USA)	18.9 m/62 ft 1 in	13.6 m/44 ft 7 in	2,180 kph/1,355 mph
JAS 39 Gripen (Sweden)	14.1 m/46 ft 3 in	8.0 m/26 ft 3 in	2,125 kph/1,320 mph
F-35 Joint Strike Fighter (USA)	15.4 m/50 ft 6 in	10.6 m/34 ft 7 in	2,000 kph/1,245 mph
MiG-25 Foxbat (Russia)	22.3 m/73 ft 2 in	14.1 m/46 ft 3 in	3,000 kph/1,865 mph
MiG-29 Fulcrum (Russia)	17.3 m/56 ft 10 in	11.4 m/37 ft 3 in	2,445 kph/1,520 mph
MiG-31 Foxhound (Russia)	22.7 m/74 ft 5 in	13.5 m/44 ft 2 in	3,000 kph/1,865 mph
Rafale (France)	15.3 m/50 ft 2 in	10.9 m/35 ft 9 in	2,125 kph/1,320 mph
Su-27 Flanker (Russia)	21.9 m/71 ft 11 in	14.7 m/48 ft 2 in	2,500 kph/1,555 mph
Tornado ADV (Europe)	18.7 m/61 ft 3 in	13.9 m/45 ft 7 in	2,340 kph/1,455 mph
Tornado IDS (Europe)	16.7 m/54 ft 10 in	13.9 m/45 ft 7 in	2,340 kph/1,455 mph

BOMBERS

Name and country	Weapons load	Length	Top speed
B-1B Lancer (USA)	34,020 kg/75,000 lb	44.8 m/147 ft	1,448 kph/900 mph
B-2 Spirit (USA)	18,145 kg/40,000 lb	21.0 m/69 ft	765 kph/475 mph
B-52 Stratofortress (USA)	31,750 kg/70,000 lb	48.6 m/159 ft 5 in	1,050 kph/650 mph
Tu-22M Backfire (Russia)	12,000 kg/26,455 lb	39.6 m/129 ft 11in	2,125 kph/1,320 mph
Tu-160 Blackjack (Russia)	16,500 kg/36,376 lb	54.1 m/177 ft 6 in	2,000 kph/1,245 mph

SPY-PLANES

Name and country	Length	Wingspan	Top speed
SR-71 Blackbird (USA)**	32.7 m/107 ft 5 in	16.9 m/55 ft 7 in	3,529 kph/2,190 mph
TR-1 (USA)	19.2 m/63 ft 1 in	32.0 m/104 ft 10 in	690 kph/430 mph
U-2A Dragon Lady (USA)**	15.1 m/49 ft 8 in	24.4 m/80 ft 2 in	690 kph/430 mph

** = no longer in service

TRANSPORT AIRCRAFT

Name and country	Maximum cargo	Length	Wingspan
An-124 Condor (Ukraine)	150,000 kg/330,695 lb	69.1 m/226 ft 8 in	73.3 m/240 ft 6 in
C-5 Galaxy (USA)	122,470 kg/270,000 lb	75.5 m/247 ft 10 in	67.9 m/222 ft 8 in
C-17 Globemaster (USA)	77,520 kg/170,900 lb	53.0 m/174 ft	50.3 m/165 ft
C-130 Hercules (USA)	19,960 kg/44,000 lb	29.8 m/97 ft 9 in	40.4 m/132 ft 7 in
CH-47 Chinook helicopter (USA)	11,340 kg/25,000 lb	30.1 m/98 ft 11 in	18.3 m/60 ft*
V-22 Osprey (USA)	6,800 kg/15,000 lb	17.5 m/57 ft 4 in	25.6 m/83 ft 10 in*

* = rotor diameter

GROUND ATTACK PLANES

Name and country	Length	Wingspan	Top speed
A-10 Thunderbolt II (USA)	16.3 m/53 ft 6 in	17.5 m/57 ft 5 in	700 kph/435 mph
AC-130U Gunship (USA)	29.8 m/97 ft 9 in	40.4 m/132 ft 7 in	480 kph/300 mph
AH-64 Apache (USA)	17.8 m/58 ft 3 in	14.6 m/48 ft*	260 kph/160 mph
AV-8B Harrier II Plus (USA/UK)	14.6 m/47 ft 11 in	9.3 m/30 ft 6 in	1,065 kph/662 mph
F-117 Nighthawk (USA)	19.4 m/63 ft 9 in	13.2 m/43 ft 4 in	1,040 kph/645 mph

* = rotor diameter

Future warplanes

Some future warplanes are already being designed and tested.
They show how warplanes might change in future.

Spy-planes without pilots

Global Hawk is a new type of spy-plane. It doesn't need a pilot –
it has computers that control its mission. It takes off, finds its own
way, completes its mission, and flies home again by itself. Without
a pilot, it can be made smaller and lighter, so it can stay in the air
for longer. Global Hawk can carry out missions lasting 42 hours.

Robot fighters

When a fighter-plane turns, the pilot is pushed into his seat. If it
turns too tightly, the forces are so strong that the pilot can faint.
A fighter without a pilot would be able to turn faster than any fighter
today. Fighters like this are called UCAVs (Unmanned Combat Air
Vehicles). This is not science fiction – the first UCAV has already
flown. A test-plane called the X-45A made its first flight in 2002.

Glossary

bomb bay space inside a warplane where bombs are carried. Most warplanes can also carry bombs and other weapons under their wings.

canards tiny wings near an aircraft's nose. Tilting the canards helps the aircraft to change direction faster, which is very important for a fighter that has to chase enemy fighters.

carbon fibre man-made material that is light but very strong

cockpit the part of a plane where the pilot sits

fighter-bomber fighter that can also drop bombs

hover to stay in the same spot while flying

jet engine type of engine that works by burning fuel to make a jet of hot gas. The jet rushing away in one direction thrusts the plane in the opposite direction.

machine gun type of gun that fires very quickly

missile weapon that is powered by a rocket. It flies towards its target and explodes.

nuclear bomb a very powerful bomb that uses energy inside atoms. One nuclear bomb can destroy a whole city. Only two nuclear bombs have ever been dropped in war. They were both dropped on Japan in 1945. Apart from their enormous power, nuclear bombs also release radiation that can kill people who survive the blast.

propeller the part of a plane that spins to move the plane through the air. Until the 1940s, all warplanes had propellers. Since then, most warplanes have been powered by jet engines.

radar a way of finding planes before they can be seen. Radar works by sending out radio waves and detecting any echoes that bounce back from an aircraft. Radar can find aircraft when they are still hundreds of kilometres away.

rotor a set of blades used by a helicopter. A rotor blade is a long, thin wing. A helicopter's engine spins a rotor very fast to lift the helicopter off the ground. Most helicopters have a smaller rotor at the end of their tail to keep the tail pointing in the right direction.

sleek smooth and slim

supersonic faster than the speed of sound. Near the ground, the speed of sound is about 1,225 kph/761 mph. High above the ground where warplanes fly, the air is much colder and sound goes more slowly. Whatever its speed is, in kilometres per hour or miles per hour, the speed of sound is also called Mach 1.

wingspan the distance across a plane from one wing-tip to the other wing-tip

Finding out more

You can find out more by looking for other books to read and searching the internet.

Books

Here are some more books about warplanes:

Designed for Success – Attack Fighters, by Ian Graham (Heinemann Library, 2004)

Fighter Planes (a Snapping Turtle Guide), by Bill Gunston (Ticktock Media, 2004)

Warplanes online

These web sites give more information about warplanes:

http://www.af.mil/factsheets – click on the name of the aircraft you want to know more about.

http://fas.org – information from the Federation of American Scientists. Click on "US Weapons Systems" and then "US Aircraft" for a list of all the aircraft you can find out about.

More to do

New warplanes are being designed all the time. See what you can find out about the new Joint Strike Fighter being built by the American plane-maker Lockheed Martin. Can you discover what is special about the US Marine Corps version? (Answer on page 32.)

Warplanes of the past

How do you think today's warplanes compare to the warplanes of the past? You can find out about old warplanes at the following museums:

◎ The National Museum of the United States Air Force (Web site: *http://www.wpafb.af.mil/museum*)

◎ The Royal Air Force Museum, United Kingdom (Web site: *http://www.rafmuseum.org.uk*)

Famous fighters of World War II include the British Supermarine Spitfire and Hawker Hurricane, the German Messerschmitt Bf-109, the Japanese Mitsubishi A6M Reisen "Zero", and the US North American Aviation P-51 Mustang.

Famous bombers of World War II include the British Avro Lancaster and the US Boeing B-17 Flying Fortress and Boeing B-29 Superfortress.

You can find out more about the P-51 Mustang fighter featured on pages 4-5 at the following web page: *http://www.wpafb.af.mil/museum/research/p51.htm*

You can also find information about record-breaking warplanes at: *http://guinnessworldrecords.com*

Index

Answer to question on page 30

The US Marine Corps Joint Strike Fighter can land vertically, like a helicopter. This means that it can land more easily on a ship.